Scrim

Scrim

Haidee Kotze

ISBN 978-0-9947104-8-2
ebook ISBN 978-0-9947104-9-9

Deep South
contact@deepsouth.co.za
www.deepsouth.co.za

Distributed in South Africa by
University of KwaZulu-Natal Press
www.ukznpress.co.za

Distributed worldwide by
African Books Collective
PO Box 721, Oxford, OX1 9EN, UK
www.africanbookscollective.com/publishers/deep-south

Deep South and the author acknowledge the financial assistance
of the National Arts Council for the production of this book

Earlier versions of some of these poems were published in
New Coin and *Illuminations 32* (special South African issue)

Cover design: Liz Gowans and Robert Berold
Text design and layout: Liz Gowans
Cover print: Willem Boshoff, 'Dromomania'
(chine-colle/letterpress)
Inside front and back covers: Detail from the same work

Contents

Smock

Always, you're
a child
with your hands lifted
&
Time
slipping its smock
over your head. Memory

games you know:
coffee, grapes,
bells, train stations
cobbled

together. All those

half-known crumbs of consonants
buttoned
at the small
of your
throat, without knowing

your body
(friable thing)
is the thread that pulls
the fabric
together:

Seasons stretched
tighter & tighter
across your chest.

Things that stay

time
pulls her black knit
over the earth,

bitter almond
on her breath.

a flood of ink
unravels in water;

the moon drops from the sky
like a rotten plum.

i summon to hand
the things that stay:

the warp of steam
rising from white skin,

potato-peel frost
on nails
in cold kitchens,

streetlights, coal,
the slide of the lock
against the night.

they come
each alone,

they care not about
the flood or after.

Up here

Up here
a gently discoloured dream
vexes at your wrists: ports

pass, time gnaws at its
own hands. Grief
drags its sleeves

through
the soup of
everything.

In the night that doesn't
stop, put your mouth
against the glass

and let your breath drop
to the spun earth, its fine
amber veins crowfooting
the dark.

Worship at the lip
of the horizon. Weep.

You're luminous –
you're a luminous brimming
balloon

haunting the radiant ceiling
of the world.

Still life

I lose time like
socks and coins, thinking
about how unknitting
you would summon doves
to throw themselves against
the window in a fit
of feathers because god-

dammit you make
my blood sing like
a buttered bell and
your shoulderblades fit in my palms

like a plateful of radishes and salt
on a table.

An old theme

the way
the light caught you there,

collaring you with
a waspy awn, i

feel this must
go the way of quince,

a sharp snap
paralysing the tongue.

despite dread
sucking at soles

we'll limp our mouthfuls
of white pebbles,

foraging after
a house to eat, not tend.

this way
the dark will catch us there,

whispering a scald of hot milk
tidily mopped up by time.

Round trip

Round and round
these mulberry
days,
the syllables
come
at a stumble
trailing
the gilt
of your words like
cat's eyes
and I
a sleeping child
on the back seat
lulled
by the lilt
of roads and shores,
a sinkful of cicadas
all sibilantly
aclutter.

I could build
a gutter
and wait for
the rain. Or

I could
summon myself like
a flotilla of rust
rising from salt
to feel the wind
lashing
its fingers
to my hair,
snapping
my spine
like a sail shuddering

the charge of
air.

Oh, this strung
thing I am,

this addle of crumbs
lisping,
in love
with teeth and scarp,
the sea spitting
at the body lithe
like butter,
so easy
to eat
for time and carp.

Round
and round again, I
simmer a reckless
rosary of steps
roughing out
the knotted bait of
the heart's
hush and
shush until

finally
I slip down
into the water

stubborn as
slate.

Web

The page is a spiderweb
a crochet of commas bargaining
for breath. I imagine

the spider at night
its sleepless spinnerets ever spooling
hopeful filament, in the morning

left for me to comb its silken code. I must
have patience with its centripetal ruses.
Slow unpicking

is the trick, the pain-
staking feeding of fibre over full stops bounding
like bobbins under the pull. The page

is a tensile bruise,
a weft of heart-bracketing glue.

Envelope

You made your mouth
an envelope

and when
I looked away

sent it through
the blinds of my ribs.

In the slipstream
of time

it flails
like a trapped

bird against a window
its wings

a semaphore
flickering against

my bones.
But up here

even feathers
have weight:

your envelope
is a lung

full of lead.
Having to choose

between breath and thrall
I ball it up

and let it fall.

Exchange

You play
schadenfreude

I raise you
self-erasing
apocrypha.

When I write
bookshelf

you read
the odds and ends
of human hands.

You give me
a buried bridge

I reply
a blank page
brimming with fossils.

You turn
them over

and I tip
inside out
wincing

my way
through the shedding

words.
We trade
trifles and trash

(number name pain)

for an abandoned skin

limpid like a lantern
blinking
on a hill.

Pith

I will lick clean
the inside
of your cheeks
shellacked with words;
        your tongue
        will fall asleep
        in my ear,
        a marrow-muscled
        elegy.
I will peel
the pith
of your bones.
        You will sprout
        under my nails,
        a graft of skin singing
        a mesocarpic shudder.
I will paddle out
to the back
of your throat
plumbing the calyx
of your skull.
        Your palate will be a raft,
        your neck
        locusts and honey,
        peaches blooming in
        a blistered waste.

In the dark hours
I am steamed open
like a pod in a wildfire
mad for seed,
        or a mussel, poor
        pithed animal
        unshelled,
        pinioned to your mouth.

I turn invertebrate
under your palms:
    a molluscular
    carpel-jointed lung.

Shuck

For the soft crook
of little knees

wasted

a poem
that puts

its small
bloody hands

insistently
around

our face.

Look,
it should say.

Look.

(The words
must be

splints

to keep
the eyes

open

dust
to keep
the tears

running.)

Feel,
it should
say.

Feel
my skin
and skull

each day
a fresh catch

of horrors
hammered

to the
horizon.

The word
is the heart's husk.

Let the poem
shuck

and shuck.

Spirograph

I drag it around

this spindly business of   lead and spoon, the

skeleton that spellbinds   windows with jasmine
and scoops rocks from   the soft fontanel of the road.

Each morning   I index moons under nails,
        offer thimblefuls of words –
wet black ink for the husks of dreams laced
        to lips like galleys spilling
hands on the milky foreheads of children
        about to boil over,
fever's firebreaks a salted trail in their necks.
        I dream

an electrical fish in your blood,   pruning your brain into
a broken bird, all bones and   pointless beak,
        and the pulling of
the body's fabric together, around,   the holding
of breath until   there is no breath to fold over, tuck under
the next,   no glue for the envelope
turning to pulp under the small furious fists
        of rain in the back garden.

Every day   upon your eyelashes
I letter my allegiance

to the dragging,   the lead ambling like a snail,
the curve of the spoon
stippled like a ghost.

Kicking

language is
is a marsh of sound

I swim through
to you

the still horizon
of your hands

keeps
me kicking

Departure

Memory wrestles spring
to the tar,

knife
against a jugular fermenting

a cumulonimbus of
syringa, wild sage, dust,

mewling rain
squalled over the horizon.

Meanwhile our spittle of words
sits seeded at the hip

breeding its silverquick sluggery:
last rites raced before dawn.

Your forehead is wound tight
with breath and oath. Still

your fine-tuned fettle
riddles your underground shell

waiting for the weight
of me.

Place oh
place

of my haunting.
How to survive

your relentless wailing wash
tripwired to my bones.

Woman with headlight

After DJ Opperman

You mount the small bonewhite
prick of consciousness to your forehead,

name it hapgood, or
some such lilted spell you can

pit against the dark
washing in from the bitter hem of the world.

Your light is a quiet orphan
etching the woodsman and his wolfish axe.

His axe hunts its hunger through the felled forest.
He swings. Coilsprings of stars

boil soft tentacles out of treetops.
The resinous blinks of small animals

fleck their fall through the ring of your light.
The stunting of it all. It snuffs your skull.

The mouth of the lake slowly clots closed in the night.
Still the tide pulls. You are mopped up by ocean,

the crunch of marsupial teeth.
From the dark the woodsman and his wolfish axe

demand a forest. Make us a forest.
Why is there no forest, wife.

You're just a spell-ridden woman
reluctantly hinged to the light on your head.

In a forest you could be a moth,
eyespots gleaming like gods on your wings.

Resurrections

You turned my dead language
with your toe.

There was gasping. A guttering of mud
from the lungs.

From among
the mourners pegged
like spindly tents against
the night

I ask

Why. The dead
are so peacefully unvoiced. Listen
to them softly simmering.

You say

I did nothing. It was you
who made it grab my ankle.
You called it up
with that larkish trill

hiding behind your teeth. Nobody heard.
Just me

and your dead language
twitching in the soil.

I say

No. You lie.
Look. Your lie squats
like a rutty toad on the roof
of your mouth. You

needed it
to speak
my names. You turned
it over, gravelly tongue
to the light. For this.
This.

No

you say. No.
Begin
again.

*

You turned my dead language
with your toe.

I say

How could I defy
the lamps of your eyes?
My words
swarm to them.

I needed it
to speak
your names

I say

I needed you
to speak my names.

Declaration

It's those multiplied maps,
declensions of time, fitfully rustling
across screens. I cannot bear

them. Their planform consolations,
platitudes against the surfeit of sky.

I shutter. In the disarticulate hours
I fold up my head. I make it
an origami marble

rolling in the jar
of your absence. I build

what I cannot live in. I hoard
what I cannot keep:

> a folly of clouds and scissors and tongues
> bombs and boxes   cruxes
> the shear of sentiment like bolts of cloth
> puckered across the sky   faces and faces
> hands and telephones and shoes   oh all   in all

the exploded views
of love pinging on the seabed.

But without time
this is no matter. I wait

for the minutes to stutter
back, their stale

breath rising
from the earth. I unfurl

my mad head. I resume.

With the morning slung to my back
I have nothing to declare

not even the heavy clockwork
of my heart.

Things to forget

Leaning into today, the road

running its hands over the spine of a time
when the future was
a mouthful of poprocks and poplar seeds

then and now fall over
each other
on this same uphill

and I remember that day when we forgot the beer
and you turned to me
and we thought about going back
but didn't.

From here
surveying the burnt world
I'd like to tell that girl:

there are worse things to forget
much more to be left behind.

Horoscope

our fortune is in the stars
sandwiched in butchered paper and days
we have buried our heads into
inhaling skin of fish   salt of chicken   oil of snake
ink and pulp   extinction soups

to be sure
we're not dead yet though soon we will be
we may yet discover piety barefooting it over three-corner jacks
or settle for a murmuration of syllables roughshod to the dawn

there is some kind of sum of years and houses
and girls and roads
I have to show my working but I've forgotten what to carry
there's always a remaindering
always fevered screws untethered across the page
injured and painfully cocked to
our soft-puddinged heart dying at a slow boil in its crock

how child-eyed to think the effervescence of sorrel
would resuscitate us
the many-fruited napes of neck countermand
our rot
sentiment is deciduous   but sorrow not

Dig

The archivist
dead in the kitchen, eyes
mothballed to
the ceiling

won't speak,
his tongue
a broken yolk
in its nest of teeth. Nothing

here to be found. Perhaps,
though, a picture
of you – your eyes oars,
or silver tacks –
tucked into

his skull, ready
to pop up like a slice of toast
at the slightest
lull. Even this

if we hold it up:
time jumping like
a trout between us, or
just a curdle of synapse
and light? Who

knows. A splash of ink
under a nail may well
give away

my heart. But we
really can't tell the disguises
of skin apart, not

without gloves and
spades. Nothing for it
then.

When they come
to dig
they'll find

you
packed tight like
a cabbage,
me
your quiet stalk.

Hummingbird postcard

i walk all day   trafficking postcards to you in my head
i drink slow-drip coffee   late into the night
watch people and birds

i'm still waking up at 4 am   part habit part hunger
all that walking in circles and also the dust in my mouth which
i keep bare and turned to the weather just in case you call
but that's a different kettle   and i need mine
to make tea for chestnut bread and tangerines on the balcony
i try not to think about endings   their tender rot
rises up from the drains

people make hummingbird love charms
roll up the poor brittle-boned dead thing in photos and names
then douse it in honey and oils   carry it everywhere
turned towards you   a little jar
of fragrant always-famished bird   echoing your heart
i've been thinking about that
the drawers of dead hummingbirds we hoard for love

anyway i should go   write when you can?
it's beginning to feel like home here
this place of guessed-at syllabaries

Twice over

We baked that cake twice
over. We'll remember

that. The Friday night. The boy
with his head over egg whites and flour
knotting the yellow light
between us. The winter evening flush
against the house. The slow

showing we save for small
hands.   This is how you measure. This is how you whip.
This is how you make your wrist do the tender work
of folding. Between us

    we showed him the slow temper of love
    while the moon brewed like a fat ball of dough over the city.

Even so, we burnt it. Not much, just

so it wasn't Right   his face said
solemn over the singed crumbs. We looked
at each other over
the kitchen   over his bright head. We said

There is more flour. And eggs and sugar. Mandarins. Oil.
It's early.

And so we baked that cake
again. We'll remember
    that.

Gift

Alas! there is no instinct like the heart –
Lord Byron, "Don Juan": Canto IV

I wanted to give you something. A mad oak tree
in a porcelain pot. Matching secateurs,
maybe. Or
a heart
like an old soft pear sugaring
in a jar. I thought about
something boxed (you
and I in a dark pantry, all floured
up). A mixing bowl. A punnet
of consonants to feed your hungry mouth,
crowds of birds clattering
at your window. A feathered language,
perhaps. But no. Too
light. Too much like
eggwhites shivering a heap of cloud
in a saucer. We're not

that. Rather then
a photograph of
the way the sea
breaks and breaks the impossible
green and blue and grey and green
of your eyes and
your salt-matted head in the shallows
of my hands. But this
never happened. Nor this –
two children earnestly bouncing light to each other
in the dusk. Still,
a mirror
for the echo of you in me? Oh

love. Beginnings are such soft-skinned things
to bite into, blanched
by time. And endings? Nobody gives gifts
for endings. We must travel light. No. Now

is the thing I wanted to give. Something for

your tart hipbone like a match
hopefully hidden in
a pocket. Something
that says the tinder of
our bodies together. Something

that burns a clean sweep of heart
right across the page.

A word minus a word

A word after a word
after a word is power.
Margaret Atwood, "Spelling"

Each day pares
the obstinate wilderness of skin
into something leaner

a thin
time a life tuned

to left-
overs words

fugitive crumbs silently swept into hands.

The palm inks and inks its
aches licks its sleeves shut
for the shelving. Each

day
is a spine chiming
with purloined pages a host
of letters fading on the tongue

each
day

prunes the hand
hungrier fingers starved

for the grammar
of things the spell that

pulls the universe like a freshly sewn pillowcase
through its own seams
into a perfectly pin-
                                        tucked
        morning.

          But
a word   minus a word   minus a word

is the sum of unsaid selves
            our shadows   briefly
doubled in a dark room:

empty   is the first language
        what is not said
cannot be lost.

Breath

A dovetail of tongues, dumb,
I think, as the sky
gravels to a halt, smog
furring its teeth.   An arm

arcs something towards us,
an answer for glass, slow-
sickled silence the thin

wire at the throat of halflinged
afternoons. Breath is all, all-

ways: bone-milk
condensed in your
mouth, your clean-
appled skull singing
in my hands.   What

fine fretworks
of skin we are, knees
fresh and fervent,   what

light lick of vowels would
be gauze enough
for the seepage of us

weeping through time.

Nightfall

the sky is a lungful of old fags
    a concoction of bird circuitries crackling
        through the mist pooling towards the riverbank
can you hear me over this?
the wind buries itself in potholes
my long divisions of follies drag their cracked heels over the grass
we're empty tins   you and I
    a harness of static biting into our aluminum ears
everything's coming up welts

the night siphons the light off into its drawers
    a turmeric wash briefly ladled into dark corners
do you remember how you used to say I was your echo?
you always were an astringent animal
    legible only to me   or so you said
        with your blonde mouth bristling on my blonde thighs
you cracked me like an existential egg

I'll leave the door ajar
  wind! salt my heart against this pulp
  this orphaned plunder
I'll leave the door ajar
will you come?   and bring inklings in a basket with my name?

the moon hangs like a hushed ball of naphthalene
    scenting the triage of us laid out on the lawn

Notes for the crossing 1

Above all,

be light. Take only

what sings
in your hand.

Shake out
your skull
like a sheet.
Let your landscapes
take flight.

As you cross

remember
to scratch your name
on the bow
against the drowned
eyes of the dead
spawning at the hull.

If they come
anyway,

set it
on fire. Don't

look back.

Swear on nothing

except
the breath
between blade and skin,

the mooring
of mulch

the sail
in your back pocket.

Still lives

A buttonhole
of quiet

in a swarm
of bees,

and so many
Monday afternoons

in a heap
at our feet.

Pines still
slouch sullen,

boys and coaldust
drag smoggy nails

along fences while
from far away

tiny skulls
keep chiming

in the wind.
God, how

these days
set like still lives,

trapdoors opening
in the sour light.

Once
we saw

an owl
on the roof,

its eyes
starched moons

we carry
like stones

or the weight
of sleeping children

in our
pockets.

Notes for the crossing 2

In the high places
slip off

this scant sock
of skin

consider
the bones

snagged around
the edges of things:

calcaneus calls
to heel

the plumbline
of the spine

phalanges
tilt pikes

against
time

talus sighs
the toss

of the die
metatarsals shill

the headlong
spill.

What shallow
twigs

to shore
this stilt of bones.

Adventure

Middle English: from Old French aventure (noun), aventurer (verb), based on Latin adventurus 'about to happen', from advenire 'arrive'.

Look.   Everything is always about to happen.
                Down by the sea
plump limpets of time cling to rocks.   Memory is indeed
a many-muscled thing: your head a palsied lightbox, blinking
through salt and sputters.

We're always just about extinct.   Unkeeled.   Which explains
how much we want to be more than
plops of feet and flowerpots, petrol stations, magazines,
parking spots.   How much we want something for the record
to show that time we saw a blue spiny cray
on the footpath   what it felt like to find a snake
drinking at the tap in the flashlight   how we chased and chased
that invisible ferrous patter running through the forest
at night.

Listen.   Things elbow at each other.   Knock, knock.   Old men
arrange their knees like knitting needles in the sun.
There is just enough rain
to keep the yard fence alive,   to keep words fluttering
at the mouth: winged pistons cranking
the rusty slow engine of the world.   Until we arrive.

Leaf

Time leafs through us
love
a lithic riffle palming a pared earth
to a perfect bare balance. You are

an orchard of planets
sown under my skin, your
sweet pear-templed sorrow swallowed by
the sea's spell. How

your plainsong spine quivered in your body
vaults the pitch and quaver of the earth to ring
a pure-tempered flint in my skull,
an incandescent burn buffed against
the dark. Time

trammels us
love
our gauge of words a fine-smocked net for flocks of scales
silver-flecked trembles
unfurled across space. Someday perhaps

I shall sail these salted seasons
with your map curled in the peat of my chest
one day
chance upon your mouth's careful chalk
a carbon cosmos
chiming in my hands.

Eventually

the shrug of objects leaves
you an uncut skein
    a silken slip of cells
    shivered over a clean bed

or so you think

you'll wake
steeped in time-drunk light
    your throat will be
    a clutter of strange birds and
    banksia seed   your eyes
    a salted jelly behind your lids

        at night
        soft-pawed animals will run
        in your ceilings

    your tongue will turn an unfamiliar fur

still
in the ransack of syllables
you'll find your skin

a well-versed thing
hemmed firmly
around your sad stock of bones

        place

        you'll see

is just a gaudy applique
crudely needled by grief

and this is all

you
and the scrim of you trussed
against tears

you'll not know
then

there is nothing but
to work

to work your heart's lumbering loom
around seeds and animals and suns

eventually
to rest
your cheek
against the slow
fray of time

Notes for the crossing 3

When you come
at last

to the country
of hours

you will find

your tongue
strung through

a shard
of ice,

the old muscle

of your heart
its sour

eye. When

at last
you come

to this,

sit. Unfurl

your sail.
Sew yourself into

the seam
of a sea

poured pure
of words.

Printed in the United States
By Bookmasters